Forsaken Fellowship

AMANDA MAREE WILSON HAGERMAN

WestBow
PRESS

A DIVISION OF THOMAS NELSON

WestBow Press books may be ordered through booksellers or by contacting:

WestBow Press
A Division of Thomas Nelson
1663 Liberty Drive
Bloomington, IN 47403
www.westbowpress.com
1-(866) 928-1240

ISBN: 978-1-4497-4560-8 (sc)

Library of Congress Control Number: 2012906024

Printed in the United States of America

WestBow Press rev. date: 04/23/2012

Contents

Thy word is a lamp unto my feet, and a light unto my path.

Psalm 119: 105

My Prayer

Lord, I am your servant; Regard my low estate;
In reverence I bow my heart; Humbled by anguish, and heartache.
From the portals of heaven look down; Let your glory rest upon our face;
Let your purpose be fulfilled; Set all things in order, and in place.
Let thy ears be attentive; Acknowledge my humble request;
That our days burst forth with laughter; and in labor our souls find rest.
Make us leap over opposition; for in victory we shall prevail;
Let us walk triumph through this valley; for it is by grace we shall assail.
May meekness guide us continually; Let unrighteousness from our home
abstain;
Make us to walk in the way peaceably; from pride we must refrain.
Our hope is anchored in you, Lord; that in these storms our soul want drift;
Standing in trust towards you, Lord; knowing you're aboard this ship.
Remove confusion far from us; Take away the dark cloudy haze;
Let truth be always before us; for truth shall enlighten the way, Amen.

By: Amanda Hagerman

CHAPTER 1

Christian Fellowship

Whenever I think about Christian fellowship, I think about a strong bond of love, and commitment between each individual. A solemn relationship that remains intact with trust and faithfulness even in the most complex moments of time. There is a staying power that holds everything together even when the storm is at its height of intensity. I also believe God desires the atmosphere to be unified and pleasant, not awkward but rather joyful and strengthening to the soul. I believe harmony should be radiant, with singleness of heart towards God and with each other.

> *"Behold, how good and how pleasant it is for brethren to dwell together in unity."*

A union of love is the most vital function in the individual life of each Christian. Yet, I have often witnessed that love isn't always the atmosphere. *"If a man say, I love God, and hateth his brother, he is a liar: for he that loveth not his brother whom he hath seen, how can he love God whom he hath not seen?-1John4:20"* God designed all of his creation with the inner capacity to love in full strength, and with that love we find an overpowering urge to unleash it to a lost and dying world. *"Freely ya have received freely give."* Love is kindled deep

1

within us, and burns like a wild fire out of control. Love consumes all hatred, bitterness, malice, envy, strife, contention, fear, and division that might try to invade, road block, or even blind us while on life's journey. It is very important that we keep ourselves in the love of God. We want to be watchmen over everyone else's soul. We recognize where everyone else is coming short but, we fail to realize where we stand. It is our responsibility to be watchmen over our own soul. Daily we need to be at work, working out our own soul's salvation with fear and trembling.

> *"Search me, O God, and know my heart: try me, and know my thoughts: And see if there be any wicked way in me, and lead me in the way everlasting. -Psalm 139:23"*

A Christian's duty is to dwell in unity with all mankind as possible. *"If it be possible, as much as lies in you, live peaceably with all men. –Rom.12:18"* This isn't always an easy task because it requires patience, and tribulation works patience, and it is through the trials that we receive the "crown of patience" (our reward for overcoming tribulation). We are called to be restorers of the waste places and to be repairers of the breech. The thing most commonly found amongst Christians should be love. Love rebuilds broken bridges and resurrects hope in times of hopelessness. Love is a foundation on which a house is built. Love has stability. Love is simply, God!! Nothing can be established without, Love! In order to be a repairer or a restorer we must first learn to walk in the full armed attributes of Love! It is than we will have something to start with, and to build on.

> *"Be kindly affectionate on to another with brotherly love; in honor preferring one another, Not slothful in business; fervent in spirit; serving the Lord; Rejoicing in hope; patient in tribulation; continuing instant in prayer; Distributing to the necessity of the saints; given to hospitality. –Rom. 12:10—13"*

There are too many "Christian P.I's"(Private Investigators) "Snoops" in the church world today. God finds them peeking around every corner trying to catch you in fault. God finds them plundering through the pages of your past trying to find some dirt on you. These are those that white glove your house, looking for something to defraud you. God calls them, 'busy bodies' or 'modern scribes and Pharisees', who always sought to find occasion against Jesus. If God wants us to know something about someone, he will reveal it to us by his Spirit, but he isn't going to confide in someone he can't trust, nor one who isn't grounded in love and compassion that can't handle the imperfections of others(the is why we aren't all an eye). But, if the devil wants you to know something he will hand deliver it to your door step by word of gossip. Because, the devil is the accuser of the brethren and his purpose, his mission, is to kill, steal, and destroy and sadly a lot of Christians have become his puppets on a string. I have noticed that amid my achievements the crowds have been small, not very many voices cheering me on. But, in my moments of failure when I messed up everyone took notice it seemed. It's as if you are utterly invisible until, you mess up. When you mess up it is than your name becomes notoriously known. A loose tongue is like a fire, inclined ears becomes its ignition; while dried up vessels are its fuel."

> *"And the tongue is a fire, a world of iniquity: so is the tongue among our members, that it defiles the whole body, and sets on fire the course of nature; and it is set on fire of hell. - James 3:6"*

Is this truly what God commissioned us to do? God said, *"Go out into the highways and hedges, and compel them to come in, that my house may be filled."* We are commissioned to preach the gospel, not spread the gossip, right? We have become so engulf with everyone else we fail to say, *"Lord, search me."* Rather than searching for the good in humanity (the God part), we incline our hearts towards only picking out the negatives. We've become so engrossed with getting the speck out of someone else's eye yet, we are reluctant to see the huge telephone pole within our own. I speak this from experience. God wants us to fix our hearts and minds upon him. Because, it is through the broken channels of fellowship with the Lord that vision, hope, love, mercy, and compassion is lost.

> *"Brethren, if a man be overtaken in a fault, ye which are spiritual, restore such a one in the spirit of meekness; considering thyself, lest thou also be tempted. -Gal. 6:1"*

Where shall I go from your Spirit? or where shall I flee from your presence? If I ascend up into heaven, you are there: if I make my bed in Sheol, behold, you are there. If I take the wings of the morning, and dwell in the uttermost parts of the sea; Even there shall your hand lead me, and your right hand shall hold me.

Psalm 139: 7–10

4

Forsaken Fellowship

Why art thou cast down, O my soul? And why art thou disquieted in me?

My soul once free like a butter fly is now unmovable as a tree.
I cry by reason of mine afflictions, thy hand doth press me sore.
I feel lost amongst great waters, and it seems I've lost my
oars.
Thy billows do rise above me, like a wall on every side.
Fear doth grip my heart, as a take view of your angry tides. Your wrath doth
kindle against me like a mighty hurricane, yet in the midst of it all I fail to call
upon your name. Thy waves do carry me farther, and farther from the shores,
and the lighthouse that once shined for me I see it no more.
Thy anchor that once held me was severed from the ship. Because when
the storms started brewing I lost hold of it. So now I am adrift in this ocean of
despair, my sails seem to be torn without any repair.
I know from whence I have fallen, failing to fellowship with thee, is why
that I am lost, amongst this raging sea. I call unto thee in the daytime, and
even unto the night. Thou come to me in on the waters, my soul doth feel
with delight. My heart doth pound within me, and my eyes do fill with tears. I
tremble and I shake, "O Lord it has been years."
You take me in your arms, and hold me even tight. You guide my little ship
through the coldness of the night.
"Remember little children in everything you do. I am only a prayer away. I will
be there for you."

By Amanda Hagerman

CHAPTER 2

Love is Pain

Throughout my life I have faced many adversities, hardships, trials, and struggles. I have tasted the bitterness of hurts, and disappointments. I have felt the pain of afflictions. I have been burnt by the flames of betrayal, and deceit wounds I thought would never heal. Brokenness I thought would never be mended. For years I have battled with this deep hurt, and discouragement of diverse kinds. Betrayal that left me wounded and bleeding; surrounding me with feelings that I felt I would never escape. Without even realizing it, people would brush up against my scabbed over wounds, and once again the pain would all come flooding back as if healing had never began. But, it was during these fragile times of emotional and spiritual warfare that God would take me back to the picture of Jesus on the cross at Calvary saying, *"father forgive them for they know not what they do."* So often I have cried out to God in my times of trouble, *"God will I ever overcome this, will I ever heal?"* Then he, the Son of righteousness arose with healing in his wings, and I found that through his enabling grace I can overcome ALL the issue in my life.

> *"The righteous cry and the Lord heareth, and delivered them out of ALL their troubles. The Lord*

*is nigh unto them that are of a broken heart: and saveth such as
be of a contrite spirit. Many are the afflictions of the righteous:
but the Lord delivered him out of them all. -Psalm34:17-19"*

In 2008 a storm started brewing in my life, and I found myself in a chaotic mess of confusion. During these days of frustration I learned to lean on God who has been my pillar of hope through it all. In brokenness I attended a prayer service at our church. I was in dire need of a touch from above. As I approached the front our church for prayer, tears dropped as rain down my face from the inward pain I released. In softness I heard these gentle words, *"Amanda, I am sending restoration into your family, I will take your family, and together you all shall walk upon the high places."* Did things go "BOOM" and magically fall together? No. To the natural eye, to the faithless, and unbelieving it seemed everything was falling apart, but I choose to trust, and believe in hope even thou it seemed hope was fleeting. Daily I waited for restoration even though I was standing amongst ruins. Was there moments of doubt? Yes. Was there frustrating days of hopelessness? Yes. Was there moments of fear? Yes. There were brief moments when the fog would settle in, but then God's voice, his promise would resound within my ears, and the shadows would flee. *"What time I am afraid I will trust in thee."* While lying in bed one night unable to sleep the Lord spoke so gently into my spirit, *"Amanda, when life presents to you its abundance of test and problems, look to me for I AM the answer."* I felt an inner peace suddenly sweep over me like a warm blanket, and I rested through the night. My conquest has been one of great lessons as I learn to walk in faith. I am learning to look beyond the natural and into the hope of a promise long waited for.

*"God is not a man, that he should lie; neither the son of man,
that he should repent: has he said, and shall he not do it? Or has
he spoken, and shall he not make it good? –Num.23:19*

In February of 2011 three years after God promised my family restoration, my husband and I separated. Had I lost hope in the restoring power of the Lord? No. It wasn't easy walking away from my home, and dividing my family. But, I felt compelled to do what I did. Things were crazy in our home from Jason's horrible drinking problem, game obsession, and our chronic disagreements that lead to fighting and arguments, and my inability to cope. I was carrying a heavy weight of guilt upon my shoulders from the selfish person I had been. My husband and I shared four wonderful children together; I realized that they had suffered tremendously on my voyage journey of waiting on Gods promise for restoration. But, all I could see was my pain; I knew it was time to take action; it was time to put my foot down on the very head of all our trouble,

> *"The God of peace shall bruise Satan under your feet shortly.*
> *-.Rom.12:20"*

I didn't walk away out of disbelief that God wasn't going to do what he said he would do. Faith requires actions and sometimes those steps of faith are the hardest ones to take because we simply do not understand them. Yet, I never stopped believing, hoping, and trusting in Gods promise. I was steadfast knowing what God said he would do, in his time.

Within the next few months things got tough. Surrounded by words of anguish, I found myself crying bitter tears of sorrow. It was a moment when I felt condemned by the forces of darkness, because I was unable to hate the one who had inflicted the most hurt upon me, and the ones I love dearly. It was a moment when I felt compelled to say, *"Lord, if loving Jason is wrong, than kill me!"* One night as I tossed the bed unrested, my tears fell in silence down both sides of my face I heard the Lord reply with such compassion, and love, *"Amanda, I loved a world that rejected me, and hated me bitterly. Yet, I died for them. So, my child, it is when you are able to love those that are unworthy of it; that you are truly loving them through me."* Confusion parted like the clouds on a sunny day, as if they were making room for the sun to shine upon me once again.

> *"Weeping may endure for the night, but joy cometh in the*
> *morning.-Ps. 30:5"*

While at McDonalds one day, I noticed that the lady working the drive-thru had a tattoo upon her neck which read, "Love is pain." Before, I would have looked at that with detestable eyes, and said, "what malarkey!" But, I didn't. It was like God was speaking to me through the words "love is pain." I began to ponder upon it with an abundance of thoughts coursing through the pages of my mind. The journey I was on had taught me something's. I could greatly recognize with the statement, "love is pain!" When I reflect on what Jesus suffered throughout his life I come to the complete conclusion that, true love is pain. Jesus endured hatred, mockery, rejection; disbelief, false accusations, betrayal, and he understood what it was like to love those that had forsaken him during his most trying moments. Yet, he died for them anyway. Could we die for the greater good of our enemies? Jesus did. Could we forgive the person that murdered our child? God did. If we are to walk as Christ walked we are going to have to suffer something's so that love can be born in us.

> *"If ye suffer for righteousness sake, happy are ye. 1Peter 3:14"*

Everyone wants to be baptized into his blessings, and grace. Rarely do you find those who are willing to be immersed in his sufferings. Why? Because, love is pain. I have come to this conclusion that if it isn't born in affliction it isn't true, Jesus being our supreme example of that. God has endowed us with the capacity for love, but the labor of love is a work that few choose to engage in. Love is tried, like faith is tried, and I have found that until you have loved those that seem unlovable, you haven't truly been acquainted with the true genuine love of God.

> *"Charity suffereth long, and is kind; charity envieth not; charity vaunteth not itself, is not puffed up, does not behave itself unseemly, seeketh not her own, is not easily provoked, thinketh no evil; Rejoiceth not in iniquity, but rejoiceth in the truth; beareth all things, believeth all things, hopeth all things, endureth all things. Charity never faileth."*

As a Christian believer I realize things can slip in at unawares so we need to daily work on our love walk above all things. We need to focus on loving those this world has tossed aside. We need to remain in complete union between our brethren, not allowing the deadly seeds of division to find root within our hearts.

> *"Follow peace with all men, and holiness, which without no man will see Lord: Looking diligently lest any man fail of the grace of God; lest any root of bitterness springing up trouble you, and thereby many be defiled.-Heb 12:14-15"*

The LORD is nigh unto them that are of a broken heart; and saveth such as be of a contrite spirit.

Psalm 34:18

Brokenness

The damage has been done; the words have been spoken,
The years have passed by, this heart is still broken.
I have used bitterness for balm; I have immersed myself in sorrow.
I waded through a valley of tears, with no hope in my tomorrow.
I have fallen into a pit; I have been swallowed up on every side,
I have stared in the face of your fury, Crippled by horrific tides.
Down on the knees of agony, anguish, and despair,
I released my pain toward heaven; you gave ear unto my prayer.
You looked down on me with comfort; you wiped away my present tears,
You healed my pain with your loving balm, you diminished my all my fear.
You anointed my eyes with salve; you bathed me with your grace,
The chambers of my heart are filled with laughter; Bitterness has lost its place.
Your presence has consumed me, in your courts I must be still,
You have given my life direction; I surrender my life for your will.

By: Amanda Hagerman

CHAPTER 3

Love's Divine Conquest

So many today act as if love is like the common cold, here today gone tomorrow, when in essence that's not love at all. 'Love' in word form is thrown out into the air so commonly in our generational time frame, we use the word 'love' so frequently as a profession of love, dedication, and commitment yet, our words often lack vigor and vitality. Jesus comprehended the lifeless, *"I love you"* and the empty promise's saying, *"Though all men shall be offended because of thee, yet I will never be offended.-Matt 26:33"* I have learned that when you come short of other people's expectations. When you stumble through life, when people come to realize just how imperfect you really are that is when you come to realize what stock they are really made of. Everyone has 'love' until you cross them the wrong way: and that is when the real truth surfaces. Love has stability, courage, and strength. Love bears deep roots that aren't easily moved by the winds of change. Love remains consistent during hardships, trials, devastation, and diversity of hurts and disappointments. *"Love never fails."*

In my mind I can envision the moment when Jesus' disciples were gathered around the table fellowshipping with him. Capturing the joy and laughter of being in the presence of the Lamb of God, *"In thy presence is fullness of joy,"* Embracing the moment. Being intrigued by every honest expression, clinging to every heartfelt word, anxiously desiring to hear more, *"Blessed are they which hunger and thirst after righteousness: for they shall be filled."* Looking steadfastly into his gentle eyes of love and compassion, having a deep knowing that something excellent and true rested behind them, Consumed by the genuine love that he exerted with every action, *"Let us not love in word, neither in tongue, but in deed and in truth."* Overwhelmed by his unfathomable grace, and virtue of his present, Chosen, handpicked, and pointed out sat these men gazing upon the countenance of the one man who felt that themselves, and the entire world was worth it all, *" he was wounded for our transgressions, he was bruised for our iniquities: the chastisement of our peace was upon him; and with his stripes we are healed."*

The disciples of Jesus walked with him, talked with him. They touched him, and ate with him. These men communed with him, laughed with him, and I am sure they cried with him also. His disciples knew him in a way that so many of us haven't. These men witnessed firsthand the devout miracles that he performed every day. He healed the sick. He fed the multitudes, and he showed compassion to those bound up in sins web saying, *"Come unto me, all ye that labor and are heavy laden, and I will give you rest."* Yet, in Jesus' most troubling and fearful hour he found no comfort from them. He said, *"What, could ye not watch with me one hour? Watch and pray, that ye enter not into temptation; the spirit indeed is willing but the flesh is weak."* Jesus warned them on the Mount of Olives saying, *"All ye shall be offended because of me this night: for it is written, I will smite the shepherd, and the sheep shall be scattered abroad."*

When the men came to take Jesus away to be crucified for the sins of the world, you see a much different picture. Instead of unified fellowship around the table, and on the Mount of Olives. You see a Savior forsaken by those whom he passionately fellowshipped with. *"Then all the disciples forsook him and fled."* In the moment when Jesus needed them the most they ran in fear, they forsook him and that is exactly how we are. When the mountain gets a little to steep for us we quit, when Gods word says, *"we can do all things through Christ which strengthens us."* When the valley is dark and long we quit, when Gods word says, *"we are more than conquerors through him that loved us."* When the storm winds surround us on every side and our ships are tossed to and fro we quit, *"O' yea of little faith."* God never quits, and God never walks away, we do. He said, *"I will never leave thee, nor forsake thee."*

One night as I laid upon my bed in the silence when everything was still; I communed with the Lord. I poured out my complaint before him, and I groaned within my lions, as tears of sorrow issued from my eyes. Surrounded by the darkness of the room, and the spiritual darkness that had bound me like bitter chains around about, I laid wrestling with the voices of my past when I heard the Lord say, *"Amanda, if all you ever see is the past than it is time to turn around, because you are walking in the wrong direction."* What God has forgiven isn't only forgiven, but it is also forgotten. It is territory even Jesus himself will not tread, and dare anyone else. Yet, what I was struggling with wasn't something I had done, but rather something I didn't do. It was a load of guilt, a cross much too heavy for me to bear. I said, *"Lord, I can't deal with this anymore."* He gently whispered," *Than let me."* Sometimes we just need to humbly lay down our boxing gloves at the feet of Jesus.

> *"Humble yourselves therefore under the mighty hand of God, that he may exalt you (lift you up) in due time: Casting all your care upon him; for he careth for you. -1Peter 5:6-7."*

Brethren, I count not myself to have apprehended: but this one thing I do, forgetting those things which are behind, and reaching forth unto those things which are before, I press toward the mark for the prize of high calling of God in Christ Jesus

Phillipians 3:13-14

Discovered

When the walls were removed,
When imperfection was revealed,
When your eyes were enlightened,
To the person I concealed.

When my thoughts became scattered,
When confusion took hold of my heart,
When the very reason for my existence,
Piece by piece was coming apart.

When my inner pain had consumed me,
Like a bone that was out of place,
I sought for comfort from your presence,
Waiting diligently for an understanding embrace.

The course of you heart shifted against me,
Your words became violent as the sea,
I trembled at your countenance,
Fear took hold of me.

You discharged yourself from my company,
You stood aloof from my pain,
You had broken the bonds of commitment,
Your heart for me had been rearranged.

The disappointment in your eyes,
Had been more than my heart could bear,
The memories daily coursed through my mind,
The laughter and friendship we shared.

I know I cannot erase the past,
But day, by day I am learning to move on,
Beyond the dark atmosphere of failure,
Into the hope of a victory won.

Each day I am stepping forward,
Trampling over the obstacles of doubt,
Obstacles have become my stepping stones,
Out of the pit from which I have crouched.

By: Amanda Hagerman

CHAPTER 4

The Cross of Unforgiveness

I have walked the bitter pathway of un-forgiveness, and I have experienced the deteriorating effects it has on one's life. Un-forgiveness damaged my relationships, crippled my health, robbed me of my joy, and made my heart hard. Un-forgiveness blinded me, and deceived me too. I would profess I had forgiven yet, my actions loudly showed attributes of un-forgiveness. My spiritual house was becoming decrepit as un-forgiveness began to take root. I bore wounds thrust from the heart of my comforters, the ones I once shared deep fellowship with. I responded with a spirit of un-forgiveness which only birthed more grief and heartache. I was embracing fire in my bosom and I was the one getting burnt. I acknowledged that I couldn't go forward in my Christian walk any longer. The fetters of un-forgiveness had brought me to a halting stand still, and it got my attention. It was as if I was standing at the brink of the Red Sea with no way across. I had a mountain on my left, and one on my right with the sound of my past roaring behind me. I knew the only way out was through the door way of forgiveness, and reconciliation. I than remembered Gods comforting words to me years prior, *"Amanda, I will part these waters that have longed troubled you, and I will make a way for you were there seems not to be a way."* Un-forgiveness is a cross even Jesus himself wouldn't bear. While on the cross he said, *"Father forgive them for they no not what they do."* Jesus resorted to forgiveness: not that forgiveness was an easy way because, it isn't. Rather because, forgiveness is the only way to God.

> *"If ye forgive men their trespasses, your heavenly Father will also for you: But if ye forgive not men their trespasses, neither will your heavenly Father forgive your trespasses. -Matt 6:14-15"*

Daily innocent people fall victim to the devices of un-forgiveness through tragedy. Tragedy falls upon a family through the loss a child or loved one to death by hands of violence. While the hand of violence suffers in a natural prison, often the victim's family suffers from a spiritual prison of un-forgiveness. God understands our frame and our frailties; he is there amongst the turmoil of tragedy and devastation. He comes with love, hope, assurance, and comfort to help us cope, if we will willingly open up the chambers of our heart to his divine love. If we will allow that love to overshadow us, and guide us through these difficult situations. It is than we will find the enabling power to overcome un-forgiveness, and soar. If we will allow God he will take all the broken pieces of our heart and put it back together with love, which is the glue that holds everything together. Love held Jesus to the cross. Love formed this world, and love is shaping your destiny.

> *"For we have not an high priest which cannot be touched with the feelings of our infirmities; but was in all points tempted like as we are, yet without sin."*

We must realize people are fallible which means: we all have the capacity to hurt, and to be hurt. The person we might perceive as, 'the picture of perfection' has most likely hurt someone, or has been hurt by someone. But, when it comes from home plate it is a blow that hurts worse than any pain we could ever experience. It doesn't mean that the individual doesn't love you, or that you do not love them. It actually reveals the closeness of each individual's heart. We might ignore a sudden blow from a distance heart: not to say it wouldn't hurt. We might even ignore the rush, and impatience of the driver who honks their horn in frustration because, we sat at a green light a little longer than they appreciated. We might even brush off an unkindly gesture from a semi social friend. But, when a blow comes at you from close range it is a deep pain like no other.

> *"For it was an enemy that approached me; then I could have borne it: neither was it he that hated me that did magnify himself against me; then I would have hid myself from him; But it was thou, a man mine equal, my guide, and mine acquaintance. We took sweet counsel together, and walked unto the house of God in company.-Ps 55:12-14"*

Let all bitterness, and wrath and anger, and clamour, and evil speaking, be put away from you, with all malice; And be ye kind one to another, tenderhearted, forgiving one another, even as God for Christ's sake hath forgiven you.

Ephesians 4: 31-32

Un-forgiveness

Through the years I have harbored feelings, of past thoughts I could not control,
Unwilling to forgive brought floods of grief into my soul.
No longer did I march forward, I stagger with fetters upon my feet,
My life was withering like a flower left out in the desert heat.
My direction was no longer clear for my heart was covered in stone,
I pounded on the doorway of heaven; the gates were locked around your throne.
I cry out to a heaven of brass, as a voice echoes back to me, saying,
"In order to be forgiven, you must forgive those who trespass against thee."

CHAPTER 5

When Love Comes Knocking

"Behold, I stand at the door, and knock if any man hear my voice and open the door, I will come in to him, and will sup with him, and he with me. -Rev.3:20"

This was a message to the church of Laodicea; the lukewarm church, the compromised church. There was absolutely nothing acceptable found amongst the Laodicea church which is so commonly seen in our day, and hour. Today we watch as the secular world finds its roots within the 'body of Christ.' Luring our young people with rock music saying, *"If we can draw them in with secularism we can preach Jesus to them,"* What? If we can draw them in with secularism than secularism can draw them right back out. *"There is a way that seemeth right unto man, but the end thereof are the ways of death. -Prov.14:12"* What happened to the body of believers who resorted to prayer and fasting until the God took notice? What happened to the 'body of Christ' doing things Gods way? We are a generation walking in a 'seem right way.' You don't bring Gods imagine down to man's level, but instead we are to bring man to Gods level. We are teaching our generation to compromise (bow) rather than instilling a spirit of Shadrach, Meshach, and Abednego within them. We are teaching them to be the tail rather than the head. This is the lukewarm church age, with Jesus standing on the outside desiring to come in.

> *"As many as I love, I rebuke and chasten: be zealous therefore, and repent. -Rev.3:19"*

Jesus' knocking reflects his importunity and patience towards his creation, which gives us a great revelation of just how compassionate and merciful Jesus truly is. Jesus stands at the very heart of humanity knocking, waiting for an invitation of fellowship. Jesus longs to share with each of us his deepest most intimate thoughts. Jesus desires to lead us into a deeper depth of his love so that we are insured an abundant life in him. Jesus wants to be that friend that sticks closer than any brother. Jesus yearns to comfort us in our times of distress and perplexity. Jesus wants to be our strength during our moments of weakness. Yet, Jesus is a perfect gentleman who will not push his way into our hearts uninvited; Jesus knocks and waits for an answer.

> *"For God so loved the world, that he gave his only begotten Son, that whosoever believeth in him should not perish, but have everlasting life.-John 3:16"*

As a child I loved church and I loved being around Gods people. It was a joyous atmosphere filled with excitement, and peace. Yet, I somehow never became acquainted with Jesus as my own personal savior. I remember seeing people touched by the divine hand of God and desiring it, but not understanding it. It excited me as I witnessed people (young people) responding to 'loves knock' with remorse while I stood in wonderment as to how I could attain, and feel what they were feeling. Even though I was too young to comprehend it fully, there was still something amazing about it. It was beautiful!

In March of 1999 three weeks after I have given birth to my second child Destiney, I was invited to a revival in Baptist Valley at Open Door Community Church by my cousin Cindy. As I walked through the doorway it was almost as if I could here, *"welcome home Amanda, welcome home."* As the worship service began I remember having a feeling in my stomach that felt like butterflies were dancing in there. Tears weld up in my eyes as the praise and worship leader sang, *"Please forgive me, I need your grace to make it through, all I have it you, I'm at your mercy. Lord I'll serve you, until my dying day, help others find a way I'm at your mercy, please forgive me."* I knew I was finally experiencing the divine presence of God's love in my own heart. As the worship service continued the preacher holding the revival asked everyone to stand to their feet because, she felt God was knocking on the doorway of someone's heart. As I stood to my feet my knees began to knock together uncontrollably. Tears steadily fell from my eyes and my heart felt as if it was going to rip clear through my chest. I was trembling under the power of God's love. Without thought I stepped out of my sit. I walked up to the precious alter and surrendered my heart and life to Jesus. I felt free, pure, and whole again. There was an excitement in my soul about life again. It was wonderful! I realized that night that my sin wasn't a barrier for God's love. Yet, Jesus didn't come to save me in my sin; he came to save me from them. That night Jesus heroically leaped over my walls of sin, and rescued my soul from the hands of death.

> *"God commendeth his love towards us, in that while we were yet sinners, Christ died for us."*

If we confess our sins, he is
faithful and just to forgive us
our sins, and to cleanse us from
unrighteousness.

1 John 1: 9

The Call

There is a call going out today all across this land,
God is trying to get our attention for his coming is at hand.
He is going around the world knocking, looking for a door that will let him in,
For the lock is on the inside of the hearts of men.
Many have rejected and turned our Lord away,
Bolted their doors with hardness, and said, "No, I can't serve you today."
But, today is the day of salvation; your tomorrow may never come,
Your hopes and dreams might fade away but, there is a forever with Gods Son.
So just get down on your knees right there were you are,
Just ask him to forgive you and come into your heart.

By: Amanda Hagerman

CHAPTER *6*

Abandoning Love's Embrace

"Nevertheless I have somewhat against thee, because thou hast left thy first love (God).-Rev 2:4"

This is a letter addressing the church of Ephesus who had abandoned love's embrace. Jesus said, *"I know thy works."* Jesus was fully conscience of their labor, patience, and discernment, but nevertheless he still had somewhat against them, because the people of Ephesus had abandoned the greatest work of all, love. Love is the beginning of all the fruits of the spirit, and of all the commandments God commanded us to follow love took the lead. Because, upon love hung the entire law, " *If ye fulfil the royal law according to scripture, Thou shall love thy neighbor as thyself, ye do well: But if ye have respect to persons, ye commit sin, and are convinced of the law as transgressors.-James 2:8-9"* If love is not the center of our labour than our labour is in vain, because in God's eyes loveless acts are counted as nothing *1Cor.13:1-8.* Without love's divine embrace upon the heart of a pastor, evangelist, apostle, prophet, teacher, worship leader, instrumentalist, or helps we might one day find ourselves saying," *Lord, Lord, have we not prophesied in your name? In thy name have cast out devils? In thy name done many wonderful works?* And then he will say," *I never knew you: depart from me, ye that work iniquity."* Why did God profess to have never known them? Because, God is love and if we do not know love, we cannot know God.

"If any man loves God, the same is known of him. -1Cor.8:3"

There is a coldness settling in amongst the church world. The fire of love we once embraced within our hearts for one another and for the lost is slowly dying. Love is God's divine tool for establishing relationships, restoring damaged walls, and repairing the broken breeches. We recognized the spiritual leak, yet instead of working to fix it so many are 'abandoning ship,' they are plummeting into the cold dark abyss of despair. *"Let love be without dissimulation. Abhor that which is evil; cleave to that which is good. - Rom.12:9"* If Christian believers are unable to cope under pressure 'abandoning ship' when things get tough. What hope will the ungodly and the sinner have?

"If the righteous scarcely be saved, where shall the ungodly and sinner appear?" In my own words, 'probably in the bars, southern exposer, or bound on diverse kinds of drugs but, not in church, and why? 'We have lost our love, our light to lead the way. Christians should be throwing this lost world a life preserver, but instead we are handing them a bag of bricks. My deepest prayer is for God to breathe upon the ambers that remain, that a fire might be rekindled within the depths of our soul once again.

"O Lord, revive thy work in the midst of years, in the midst of the years make known: in wrath remember mercy.-Hab 3:2"

One day while I was praying I heard God say, *"Amanda, I have sealed you with the Holy Spirit of promise"* as his gentle words overshadowed my inner fear, tears issued like rivers down both sides of my face. In my spirit I could see a golden seal resting upon my head. God said, *"Amanda, this is my covenant with you, my seal, my promise, to never leave you nor forsake you, and to redeem you on redemption day."* I felt his love and comfort surrounding me as a warm soft blanket. God said, *"Amanda, this covenant can only be broken by you, for I have preserved you."* Then I saw the faces of people that I knew who once walked in victory, power, and love, but upon their heads rested broken seals, because they had abandoned love's embrace.

> *"Ye did run well; who did hinder you that ye should not obey the truth? -Gal.5:7"*

Can you remember the day when you became acquainted with your 'first love'? I do! I remember the joy and excitement I felt way down deep inside of my heart and soul. I remember being so focused that my 'first love' was all I could ever think about. I remember getting butterflies in my tummy just from the mention of his name. I remember wasting countless pieces of paper simply because I wanted my message of love to be perfect and clear without out any doubt. I remember how anxious I got when the phone would ring at our house because; I couldn't wait to hear his voice on the other end. Do you remember how overwhelmed you became when you were finally able to stand in the presence of the one you adore? I do! I remember feeling absolutely complete. Yet, as times passes on, and days become years we often find ourselves taking our 'first love' for granted. Instead of those feelings blossoming into a beautiful rose garden with deep roots, they slowly began to fade. When love in any relationship whether God-ward or man-ward isn't nurtured, cultivated, and watered it will eventually die from neglect.

Our relationship with our natural 'first love' sometimes reflects our relationship with God our spiritual 'first love'. We start out as a revolutionary, we're determined, confident, strong willed, and bold. Than the honeymoon is over, and suffering settles in, and we find that our relationship is spiraling from neglect, because our will to fight is gone. *"How shall we escape, if we neglect so great salvation? -Heb.2:3"* So many Christians have walked away from their commitment with God their 'first love' abandoning the only one who can help them when no one else can, leaving them surrounded by only the memories of love's divine embrace.

> *"I am come that they might have life, and that they might have it more abundant.-John 10:10"*

Do we only have a remembrance, or is our walk with God still a reality? Do we only have a remembrance of the fire we once had, or do we still embrace it? Do we still get those butterflies of excitement when we enter into the gates of the Lord's house, or is it only a remembrance of what was? Do we still run into the arms of God's loving presence when trouble emerges, or are we finding ourselves running away? Do you see where he brought you from, or are you only seeing where you use to be? In my spirit I can hear God calling out to out remembrance saying, *"Remember therefore from whence thou are fallen, and repent, and do thy first works."*

If the Son therefore shall make you free, you shall be free indeed.

John 8:36

Captured

I am destitute of water, for the well within my soul,
Is broken through tragic mishaps, now no water will my vessel hold.
I have sold myself for naught, traded wisdom for bags with holes,
I have mingled my drink with poison; I have dealt treachery to my soul.
I have danced to the music of death, and eaten from the table of deceit,
I stumbled through the darkness, as sin wraps round my feet.
I have shaken the hand of the enemy; I have embraced a sinful cause,
I have walked in the way of my own counsel; I have not recognized or
acknowledged your laws.
I am compasses by bar without, I am enclosed by walls within,
I am held captive by voices of doubt; I am imprisoned in bonds of sin.

By: Amanda Hagerman

CHAPTER 7

Love's Ambassador

*"For the law is fulfilled in one word, even in this;
Thou shalt love thy neighbor as thyself. But if ye
bite and devour one another, take heed that ye
be not consumed one of another. This I say then,
Walk in the Spirit, and ye shall not fulfil the lust
of the flesh. -Gal. 5:14-16"*

As ambassadors of God we should never lower ourselves to ambassadors of mass destruction. We are commissioned by God to destroy the works of Satan, but not the people under his power. Satan will often divert our attention upon the problems, rather than the answer which is God. We are called forth as ambassadors of Christ to love, and pray for those who have been entrapped by Satan's ploy. That by prayer, love, and the word of God we might through God destroy the strongholds, and devices of Satan. *"For we wrestle not against flesh and blood, but against principalities, against powers, against the rulers of the darkness of this world, against spiritual wickedness in high places.-Eph. 6:12"* Our enemy is the unseen factor in the equation, and Satan makes it a point of remaining unseen while he sits back with great delight as we yield ourselves to his devices, destroying one another with words and unprofitable worldly tactics.

> *"For though we walk in the flesh, we do not war after the flesh :(For the weapons of our warfare are not carnal, but mighty through God to the pulling down of strongholds ;) Casting down imaginations, and every high thing that exalteth itself against the knowledge of God, and bringing into captivity every thought to the obedience of Christ; -2Cor.10:3-5"*

David was a mighty ambassador for God. David and his men rested in a cave in the strongholds at Engedi. Saul, David's adversary who sought to take David's life was on the prowl in the hills of Engedi, when Saul blindly decided to rest in the very cave David and his men was dwelling in. David's men said, *"Behold, the day which the Lord said unto thee, Behold, I will deliver thine enemy into thine hand, that thou mayest do to him as it seem good unto thee."* David was given an advantage over Saul, for God had delivered Saul into David's hands. Instead of David reacting with a rash hasty spirit, David showed compassion, and godly fear coupled with abundant mercy, proving to be a man after 'God's own heart.' In Ps. 26:2 David prayed unto the Lord, *"Examine me, O Lord, and prove me, try my reins and my heart."* So, could this have been a test to see what was within David's heart? Sometimes I believe God allows things to enter into our 'secret places' our 'comfort zones' only to prove us to see how we will respond. Will we reacting with a rude, self-centered, rash, arrogant or vengeful spirit? Or, are we reacting with love, compassion, gentleness, meekness, longsuffering, and forbearance? David was given the power to destroy, yet he laid aside vengeance and armed himself in mercy.

> *"Put on therefore, as the elect of God, holy and beloved, bowels of mercies, kindness, humbleness of mind, meekness, longsuffering; forbearing one another, and forgiving one another, if any man have a quarrel against any: even Christ forgave you, so also do ye. And above all these things put on charity, which is the bond of perfectness. -Col.3:12-14"*

David often prayed for God's vengeance upon his foes. *Ps.71:13 "Let them be confounded and consumed that are adversaries to my soul; let them be covered with reproach and dishonor that seek my hurt." Ps. 69:22 " Let their table be a snare before them; and that which should have been for their welfare, let it become a trap."* David was a man acquainted with grief. David shook hands with sorrow, and stood in the face of adversity. David embraced sin, and knew the agony that came from God's angry hands of chastisement that humbled him, because God loved David. David acquired a great tenderness towards God for he was a repentant man who showed ample amounts of mercy; as seen in the situation with Saul his adversary. The book of Psalms reveals diverse sides of David from bitterness, anger, and grief issuing from his words: To compassion, mercy, and tenderness which reveals David inward struggle between the forces of bitterness, hatred, and un-forgiveness, and the power of God's love, mercy, and forgiveness. Have you ever been there? I have. There have been moments in my life of deep distress, and painful affliction. I have often felt compelled to pray unmerciful prayers as David did. Yet, I would always feel a gentle tugging in my spirit from God that pulled me right back to mercy, recalling the abundance of grace, and mercy God's extended to me throughout my years of 'short comings.' We must remember that as Christians we aren't any better than the sinner man or women, we are just better off.

> *"For I say, through the grace given unto me, to every man that is among you, not to think; of himself more highly than he ought to think; but to think soberly, according as God hath dealt to every man the measure of faith.-Rom.12:3"*

For by thee I have run through a troop; and by my God have I leaped over a wall.

Psalm 18: 29

Overcoming

With the winds of change that is blowing all across our lands, bringing the
image of God's name down to the status of man.

I will stand and be bold, I will embrace the cross, and I will teach the infallible
truth to a world that is lost.

I want bow to their gods, nor be altered by their faith, I will walk through the
fire, in the power that He delegates.

I will be strong in the truth, and the power of His might. He is my arm of
Victory in my battles He will fight.

I will march through a troop for he is on my side. I will run for He's my fortress
in His pavilion I will hide.
I will fight in the midst of the battle, my enemies He will subdue, for through
Him I am a victor and with Him I will never loose.
He's my present help in trouble; He's my strength in the midst of my pain.
He's my friend that is closer than a brother, and in Him I find great gain.
He's my joy in the midst of sorrow; He's my courage in the midst of fear.
He's my comfort in the midst of chaos, and my guidance if I will hear.

By: Amanda Hagerman

CHAPTER 8

Love's Divine Treasure

"A little that righteous man hath is better than the riches of many wicked. -Ps.16"

While I was lying in bed one early morning I was thinking about all of the failures, and disappointments I have encountered. As I looked around the unfinished room I had been sleeping in, I pondered deeply upon all the imperfections around me. I murmured in silence within my own heart, as I felt as if the table of blessing had been turned to cursing within our lives; when the Lord spoke to me so gently, *"Amanda, the soul that is void of love, is one stricken with poverty."* It was then realized if I gain the entire world and all of its worldly goods, and never acquire love than in essence I haven't gained anything at all. Love is the divine treasure that is often overlooked amongst the worldly splendor of ' things.'

" Because, thou sayest, I am rich, and increased with goods, and have need of nothing; and knowest not that thou are wretched, and miserable, and poor, and blind, and naked.-Rev.3:17"

According to this world's estimation I have nothing, and according to US standards my family and I live below poverty level. Yet, my family and I do not live in accordance to this world's economy or standards, but according to God's. In God's economy I am an heir to the throne of heaven, but to this world I am nothing more than the dirt under some people's feet. I am not decked with silver and gold. I do not have more money that I need. Most of my worldly attire is second hand. I am not endowed with an abundance of worldly riches, and I struggle every once in a while. Yet, I am blessed, because my treasure, my hope, my promise isn't amongst 'things' rather it lays way beyond the portals of this world, protected.

> *"Lay not up for yourselves treasures upon earth, where moth and rust doth corrupt, and where thieves break through and steal; But lay up for yourselves treasures in heaven, where neither moth nor rust doth corrupt, and where thieves do not break through nor steal: For where your treasure is, there will your heart be also.-Matt 6:19-21"*

Lazarus was a beggar who laid daily before the rich man's gate, desiring nothing more than the crumbs that fell from the rich man's table. Yet, the only comfort he found was from some nearby dogs who came and licked his wounds. Everyday this rich man passed by Lazarus unmoved by Lazarus's disposition; never extending a hand of compassion, nor showing any remorse for the welfare of Lazarus. Than the tables turned, One day Lazarus died and was carried by the angels into the arms of God where he was comforted, and at rest. But, the rich man died and in hell he lifted up his eyes in torments, begging for just a drop of water to cool his parched tongue, and no compassion was given unto him.

> *"But whoso hath this world's good, and seeth his brother have need, and shutteth up his bowels of compassion from him, how dwelleth the love of God in him? My little children let us not love in word, neither in tongue; but in deed and in truth.-1Jn. 3:17-18"*

This world might overlook your disposition; it might view you as a burden to society. Amongst this world you might feel forgotten and often trampled underfoot, by the scribes and Pharisee of our modern times. You might lack Hollywood glamour, and prestige, but remember!

Jesus Christ Savior of the entire world, love's divine treasure didn't come arrayed in the attire of a king, yet he was. Jesus was born in a humble stable amongst the animals. Jesus was found wrapped in swaddling clothes lying in a manger, and never once have I read where Mary ever complained or showed discontent. Jesus' birth was herald by a multitude of heavenly host crying, *"Glory to God in the highest, and peace on earth good will toward men,"* and his death was proceeded by an angry crowd crying, *"Crucify! Crucify! Crucify!"*

> *"If the world hate you, ye know that it hated me before it hated you. If ye were of the world, the world would love his own: but because you are not of the world, but I have chosen you out of the world, therefore the world hateth you. - Jn.15:18-19"*

The fear of the LORD is the beginning of wisdom: and the knowledge of the holy is understanding.

Proverbs 9:10

Prayer for Wisdom

Wisdom, guide my steps,

Wisdom, led my heart,

Wisdom, be my eyes that I might find refuge in the dark.

Wisdom, be my friend,

Wisdom, guard my mouth,

Wisdom, direct my conversations that words of ignorance do not spill out.

Wisdom, be my discernment,

Wisdom, open my ears,

Wisdom, is calling out to me if only I will hear.

Wisdom, teach me to be a good daughter,

Wisdom, teach me to be a good friend,

Wisdom, teach me to be a good mother, a listener to all of them.

Wisdom, teach me to be a good follower,

Wisdom, teach me how to lead.

Wisdom, teach me to walk in your love, so I will be a sower of perfect seed.

Wisdom, be my joy,

Wisdom, be my peace,

Wisdom, be my laughter in the midst of these raging seas.

Wisdom, be my pilot,

Wisdom, guide my soul,

Wisdom, steer my finances, that I may prosperously reach my goals.

Wisdom, be within my walls,

Wisdom, be the foundation on which my house is built,

Wisdom, be the stability that my house will not tilt.

Wisdom, give me grace to face this adversity,

Wisdom, allow me to rise from the ashes of fear, and anxiety.

Wisdom, be my courage.

Wisdom, become my feet,

Wisdom, consume my being, that in you I will have victory.

CHAPTER 9

Power of Words

"The thief cometh not, but for to steal, and kill, and to destroy: I am come that they might have life, and that they might have it more abundantly. Jn. 10:10"

We often categorize sin into divisions, 'BIG sins" v/s 'little sins.' When in all reality there aren't any categories at all, because sin is simply that, sin. Sin is the manifestation of an inward thought that became an action, or a weakness within our flesh that over road our ability to reason. That is the reason God's word says, *"Be strong in the Lord, and in the power of his might."* All the consequences of unrepentant sin is eternal death whether 'little' or 'BIG.' The message of the murder is loud, and blares across our public airways. We never think twice about praying for God to comfort the victim's family. We make every attempt possible to reach out to them, to help them shoulder this burden and it is vital that we do so. But, how many feel compelled to cry out for God's salvation, love's divine intervention upon the sin stricken life of the victimizer? We might put murders in the 'BIG' category because we seem to always notice the 'BIG' things, but we tend to overlook the 'little things', but God doesn't. Just because I made a choice while in the world to dance in the shallow waters of sin, was I heading to a different destination than those who choose to launch out into the deep?

One night as I lay upon my bed enjoying the peace, and quietness around me, I found myself engaged in deep thought, when I heard these words," *It isn't only the big things that have sent mankind to hell, it is the little motives, and the little thoughts of man's hearts that have sent them there to, it is the little foxes that spoil the vine."* The murders message comes in like thunder, and everyone takes notice, yet what about the 'secret sins' the 'little sins' people are committing daily? *"Whosoever hateth his brother is a murderer: and ye know that no murderer hath eternal life abiding in him. -1Jn.3:15"* People quietly, and secretly slander, and tear down one another with the tongues through gossip, and lies. It doesn't take a knife, a gun, a fist, or a US military weapon to destroy someone, all it takes is one solitary word.

> *"Death and life are in the power of the tongue: and they that love it shall eat the fruits thereof. -Prov.18:21"*

When the word of God is stood upon, believed, lived by, and spoken with authority, it has the power to make us overcomers (the head). But, when we doubt the word, reject the word, walk against the word, trample the word, and refuse to apply the word. God's words than obtains the power to sentence us to eternity in hell, making us the tail. As a child growing up the saying was, "sticks and stones may break my bones, but words will never hurt me." As an adult I have found this saying to be far from truthful, and incorrect. Words are powerful! Words have the ability to take the spirit of mankind to a higher level, but words also have the ability to bring the spirit of mankind into utter depression. King David referred to words as weapons. David put words in the bow, arrow, sword, and spear 'category.'

> *"My soul is amongst lions: and I lie even among them that are set on fire, even the sons of men, whose teeth are spears and arrows and their tongue a sharp sword. -Ps. 57:4"*

> *"Who whet their tongues like a sword, and bend their bows to shoot their arrows, even bitter words: That they may shoot in*

secret at the perfect: suddenly do they shoot at him, and fear not. Ps.64:3"

David being a man of war, and battle expressed that words are as painful as the wounds experienced from a sword, arrow, and spears.

"No weapon that is formed against thee shall prosper; and every tongue that shall rise against thee in judgment thou shalt condemn. This is the heritage of the servants of the Lord, and their righteousness is of me, saith the Lord. - Isaiah 54:17" Words are weapons that we form within our mouths against those we hate, or are angry with making them our target, and our words darts. When words of anger are issued from our hearts they become fiery darts aimed with a strong purpose to subdue those that have afflicted us, and this is not God will for his children.

"Be angry, and sin not: let not the sun go down upon your wrath: Neither give place to the devil. -Eph. 4:26-27"

We are to stand against these spiritual weapons in faith, using the word of God as our defense, our strong tower, our fortress, and our way of overcoming spiritual warfare, as Jesus demonstrated. Paul referred to words as, open sepulcher, and the poison of an asp. The bite from the asp was the least terrible way to die; the venom brought sleepiness and heaviness without spasms of pain, yet the end result was fatal.

"Their throat is an open sepulcher; with their tongues that have used deceit; the poison of asp is under their lips. Whose mouth is full of cursing and bitterness. -Romans 3:13"

It is as if the church world has been crippled with the poison of the asp. Slowly we are drifting away from reality into a world of slumber. *"While men slept, his enemy came and sowed tares among the wheat, and went his way."* It has been while we were sleeping that the enemy has stolen our treasures of hope, peace, joy, zeal, faith, healing, strength, power, desire, focus, rest, salvation, children, and above all our love. Yet, we would most likely put 'words' in the 'little sin' category, when people's words have destroyed more homes, lives, relationships, and churches than any natural weapon.

Jesus exemplified the power of words as he walked by cursing the unfruitful fig tree, and presently the fig tree withered away. Jesus spoke to the angry waves, and they cussed. Jesus spoke the word and people were healed. Jesus rebuked demons and they took flight. Jesus spoke and people believed, and were converted. Jesus spoke and sins were forgiven. Jesus spoke and life entered into vessels where death had taken up its abode. Jesus proved that his word has the power to change things, fix situation, heal sickness, calm storms, and rebuke hindrances. Words are powerful!

> *"Let the words of my mouth, and the meditation of my heart, be acceptable in thy sight, O Lord, my strength, and my redeemer. Ps.19:14"*

When I was in the first grade of school I found myself struggling to achieve. Yet, I wasn't being mentored by someone who believed in me either. I had become the focus of laughter, and mockery amongst my classmates which was initiated by my leader, my teacher, and my guide. Daily I was pointed out as, "the failure." The only position I was given was to stand in the back of the line, because "failures had no place in the front." His words and his laughter wounded my fragile spirit. For years I saw myself as, 'the failure.' I could never quite grasp his hatred towards me, and his un-wiliness to except me like he did others. This man was a father, a doctor, and a teacher who had taken the seat of influence in so many young lives. Within his hands was given the power (as a doctor) to heal, yet he was wounding. Rather than embracing the power to teach, guide, care, love, and encourage our generation to excel. He belittled, and embraced the power to mislead. He might have acquired the greatest height of a degree, yet lacked the greatest one, love, compassion, understanding, care, and wisdom. I wasted countless years trying to shape myself into everyone's category of approval, just because someone in authority didn't believe in me. Words are powerful!

> *"Speak evil of no man, to be no bawlers, but gentle, shewing all meekness unto all men. For we ourselves also were sometimes foolish, disobedient, decieved, serving divers lusts and pleasures, living in malice and envy, hateful, and hating one another. Titus 3:2-3"*

Submit yourselves therefore to God. Resist the devil, and he will flee from you.

James 4:7

Bitterness

When bitterness entered in, like the poison of an Asp; my inner chambers
became hard as stone;
Love, mercy, and compassion made a swift escape, in fear and darkness my
soul did roam.
Deceit rested under my tongue; Guile was expelled from my lips;
My mind became an inventor of hatred, towards mischief my feet ran swift.
My hands became tools of destruction; my ears were inclined to lies;
My loins had filled with corruption; blindness settled over my eyes.
Your love pounded upon me; I broke like a dam bursting through a gate;
One word of your infinite truth; Redirected my eternal fate.
You renewed my strength like the eagles; as I opened wide the chambers of my
heart;
Love, Mercy, and compassion returned; Like the warmth of a fiery dart

By: Amanda Hagerman

CHAPTER 10

When Loves Reaches Down

"God sent not his Son into the world to condemn the world; but that the world through him might be saved. -Jn.3:17"

Maybe you are one of those that life has left you feeling worthless and useless? Or maybe you feel as if you are beyond love's reach, because you have taken a nose dive into the cesspool of sin? We must remember when we wonder off and get lost God is always fully aware of your location, and at the sound of your cry he will leave the ninety and nine to come after that one lost lamb. You are precious. You are what Jesus came for, and God has a plan for your life. You were designed with a purpose that pointed towards Calvary (eternal life), not destruction. Some people feel that they were born hell bound, but this is a lie from Satan. Failure has been imprinted upon so many young lives, because no one ever believed in them. All they ever received was ridicule, rather than anyone ever recognizing their inner treasure. And sadly this is very prevalent amongst Christian homes. Yet, you can find comfort in knowing God believes in you or he wouldn't have created you, nobody believes more in their product than the manufacturer.

> *"For I know the thoughts that I think toward you, saith the Lord, thoughts of peace, and not of evil, to give you and expected end. -Jer. 29:11"*

The secular world is so tired of our religion, our programs, and our formalities that don't offer a cure to the sin sick souls of humanity. We hammer the importance of change only offering them a conversion to manmade laws, and regulations, but God desires an inward change of one's heart. The secular world is hungry for one thing, boundless unconditional love. Love that doesn't overlook the flooding issues of sin, but rather than inflicting more pain upon it: 'true love' becomes the ointment. The secular world is full of criticism, hatred, betrayal, and condemnation, but we (the Christians) are to be like the Good Samaritan. When the world has kicked people down, we should undergird them with love. When this world has trampled people, we should be that shoulder of love they can depend on. When this world has condemned, criticized, and judged, we should be that word of love, comfort, and hope. We are the body of Christ, or are we? Jesus is more than a list of rules, and regulations. Jesus desires a relationship with his creation, with bonds and chains of love, faithfulness, and commitment, and nothing more.

> *"Thou shalt love the Lord thy God with all thy heart, and with all thy soul, and with all thy mind. This is the first and great commandment. And the second is like unto it, Thou shalt love thy neighbor as thyself. One these two commandments hand all the law and the prophets.-Matt. 22:37-40"*

If someone isn't living to soot our standards, instead of us consistently telling them they have a problem all the time, we need to show them the remedy, because the sick know they are sick. It is the cure they need not someone's idea, opinion, judgment, or condemnation. Rather they need our prayers, and love. Instead of us casting stones, and pointing fingers like modern 'scribes and Pharisees' we should be pointing them towards Calvary. One day while Jesus was in the temple teaching, the scribes and Pharisees 'the religious sect' interrupted him by bringing unto him a woman taken in adultery, and they were ready to stone her to death. Jesus saw her as a hand full of purpose, rather than a menace to sociality. I imagine Jesus saying, *"This is what I came for."* We are so quick to see the error within someone's life, when not one of us is the ideal of perfection; we have all sinned and come short of Gods glory. Before we gather our stones of judgment making people our target, let's remember that we were once a servant of sin when God extended his hands of love and mercy towards us. Jesus said unto her, *"Woman, where are those thine accusers? hath no man condemned thee? She said, No man, Lord. And Jesus said unto her, Neither do I condemn thee: go, and sin no more."*

In my life I have made an abundance of blunders, and mistakes. I am far from the emblem of perfection. But, everything I have did, been through, and seen has been for my perfecting (maturing) in Christ. I have not always reacted with love in difficult situations. I have had stones threw at me, and I have picked them up and threw them right back. I have not always been trustworthy either, but everything has been to teach me that I am never alone, even when I have felt utterly forsaken by those I love the most. In the mist of depression God has been my strong tower. In the storms he has been my rock, my stability, and my peace. I have learned not to judge things as I see them, but to look deeper past the marred imagine of humanity, because that is where the true heart is. To this world you may be nothing but to God you are a treasure. You aren't just a mere existence, you have a purpose!

> *"The Lord is not slack concerning his promise, as some men count slackness; but is longsuffering to us-ward, not willing that any should perish, but that all should come to repentance. -2Peter 3:9"*

Come now,
and let us reason
together, saith the
LORD:
though your sins
be as scarlet, they
shall be as white
as snow; though they
be red like crimson,
they shall be as
wool.

Isaiah 1:18

Stoning Judgment

With condemning accusations you crushed my wounded soul,
Trampled the shattered broken fragments, rather than offering balm that I
should be whole.
With stretched forth fingers you acknowledged my sin that brought me shame,
Casting forth your stones of judgment, you brought great sorrow to my pain.
You paraded my transgressions like a trumpet preparing for battle,
I was left gasping for air, searching for strength, slowly I became unraveled.
Surrounded by accusers, my haters, my enemies,
Bound in the walls of my own prison crying, "O' Lord please set me free."
God gave ear to my feeble cry; I was broken, bleeding, and ready to die.
God, you illuminated me with your love, you reached way down to pick this
unworthy soul up.
You rescued my soul from the clutches of sin,
You cast away the stones that I was condemned with.
You released me from the shame, and the sins openly shown.
You said, *"Now, let him that is without sin, cast the very first stone."*

By: Amanda Hagerman

CHAPTER 11

Love's Perfecting Power

"Study to shew thyself approved unto God, a workman that needeth not to be ashamed, rightly dividing the word of truth. -2Tim.2:15"

As my pastor has often said," There is no such thing as a stupid question, IF we have the answer to it." And as my mother has always said," If you never ask, you will never know." So do not ever be afraid to ask a question if you do not understand something. There is simply nothing wrong with ignorance (being unlearned), it is staying that way that is a shame. I can't say I am perfect (mature spiritually) in every area, but I can say I am eager to learn more. Daily I am taking up my cross and following him through prayer and the word of God. I live daily in the light that I have, and I walk in the understanding that I have obtained. I know that if I apply myself, and study to show myself approved, when times of testing comes to my door I want have to fear failure or be ashamed. But, if I haven't applied myself in faithfulness towards the welfare of my soul, I want be prepared when times of testing, trouble, chaos, and confusion arises. When we fail to study Gods word, and submit ourselves in fervent prayer, we aren't letting God down, we are letting ourselves down. God demands growth, and desires to promote us, but he can't unless we are engaging ourselves. Jesus wants us to have knowledge and understanding of his truth, and it is the knowledge of that truth that has the power to make you free.

> *"Ye shall know the truth, and the truth shall make you free.*
> *-Jn.8:32"*

So many of God's army have surrendered in the heat of conflict against these raging powers of Satan, because they haven't attired themselves in the 'whole armor of God' When God's armor enables us to stand against Satan's wiles, and devices. If we do not understand the truth of God's word, than we become vulnerable to Satan's vicious lies. The entire armor consists of God's infinite truth, yet through lack of understanding and knowledge Satan gains the advantage on God's army. It isn't always out of inability to understand the truth, but through slackness in using the resources God has given us. Our greatest resource being: 'The Comforter' 'The Holy Spirit' who will lead us and guide us into all truth. It is through the breech of slackness Satan makes entry, crippling God's warriors through the 'doorway of ignorance.'

> *"Submit yourselves therefore to God. Resist the devil, and he*
> *will flee from you. - James 4:7"*

God doesn't just call the educated, rather he educates the called. No born again believer starts out with a twelfth grade education, nor would you take a toddler and place them in a collage university. People don't go from the alter of surrender; to the pulpit of service in one day; just as people don't plant a garden and wake up the next day to a field of crops. Rather it is after months of nurturing, watering, cultivating, and care, that you than see the finalized product of your labor. We don't start out on top of everything, because growth is gradual. We start off taking one baby step of faith at a time. As we grow in Christ we will mature through understanding and knowledge until we become perfected (mature).

> *"All scripture is given by inspiration of God, and is profitable*
> *for doctrine, for reproof, for correction, for instruction in*
> *righteousness: That the man of God may be perfect, throughly*
> *furnished unto all good works. -2Tim.3:16-17"*

Several years ago in 2003 God visited me in a dream. I dreamed I was skipping through a field that I played in when I was a little girl. I remember feeling such peace and harmony within my soul, and the sun in all its brightness didn't sting my skin, rather it soothed it. Everything sparkled around me. Then I came upon a group of little lambs which were eating something that smelt very foul. I remember thinking a wolf was nearby, because only a wolf would do this. I remember becoming very alert, and watchful. Then he appeared before me black as coal, and vicious. He lunged at me with a fury. He took hold of my arm with his teeth, and in Jesus name I rebuke him and he went flying out of sight, but quickly appeared again. Three times I faced him and the third time as I was rebuking him, I bumped into something behind me, and I know who it was. As I reverently turned around I beheld a white garment standing behind me, it was like nothing I have ever seen. As I slowly looked up to behold his face it was hidden within the clouds. But, I heard a voice say, *"Amanda, let me handle this it is too big for you."*

God knew one day I would shepherd a small flock of little lambs, and he saw within me a heart of a leader something I didn't see within myself. God knew the struggles I was going to undergo, and the fight I was going to have. Through the years I have witnessed as young people have traded destruction for eternal life. I have seen young people hold on during difficult times, and struggles. I have seen them standing bold against the strategies of satanic influence. But, I have also witnessed the overwhelming fight to keep them on board the ship of life, as some slowly shrieked back into the ways of unrighteousness plunging out into the world of 'hungry shark infested waters.' It has been heartbreaking and utterly devastating at times. But then I remember God words saying, *"Amanda, let me handle this it is too big for you."* Goliath was too big for David, but he wasn't too big for the God David served. Through the years God has taught me that I can't change everything, but to change what I can. If I minister to thirty young people, and four take root than I need to be thankful for those four, but never stop praying for the twenty-six who went astray.

"Humble yourselves therefore under the mighty hand of God, that he may exalt you in due time: Casting all your care upon him; for he careth for you. -1Peter 5:7"

Yea, though I walk through the valley of the shadow of death, I will fear no evil: for thou art with me; thy rod and thy staff they comfort me.

Psalm 23:4

Never Alone

While walking through the valley, I lift my hands up towards the sky,
I watch as storm clouds erupt into sunlight, as I surrender my will for thine.
Your glory descends down upon me, like tiny droplets of rain,
My weariness falls like shackles; your love consumes my inner pain.
Your arms enfold about me, like the warmth of the sun,
You have undergirded my soul with strength, when the race was hard to run.
You have captured me in your presence; you have surrounded me with your grace,
You have overwhelmed me with your mercy; you shined upon me with your face.
I am dancing in your field of lilies, I am rejoicing on your mountains high,
I am lifting my voice towards heaven; I am spreading my wings for now I must fly.

By: Amanda Hagerman

CHAPTER 12

Unveiling Your Potential

Maybe you are one of many that has been beaten, battered, and abused by life's unexpected occurrences, and it has left you feeling insignificantly worthless. Your excursion has taken you down a long pathway to nowhere, simply because your potential was never unveiled, recognized, or acknowledged but your short comings were. You feel like you have been immersed into a world of negativity and your drowning in a sea of doubt. Yet, just as God lifted up Simon Peter as he began to sink in the midst of the boisterous storm, God will rescue you from the clutches of doubt, and fear that has been pulling you under if you will simply acknowledge him. If you will cry out to him and recognize that HE IS your very present help in times of trouble. HE IS a friend that sticks closer than a brother. HE IS your refuge in the midst of chaos. HE IS there to comfort in the hour of brokenness and sorrow. And HE IS our confidence when we are surrounded by a world of negativity, and ridicule.

> *"In my distress I called upon the LORD, and cried unto my God: he heard my voice out of his temple, and my cry came before him, even into his ears.*
> *-Ps. 18:6"*

One night at prayer meeting I came with a shattered spirit, crushed by words of confusion and hurt, yet in the midst of it all I could still feel that gentle loving touch from above letting me know I wasn't alone. As we came forth for praise and worship I just felt the need to stand still. As I stood with hands lifted high I could feel his presence rejuvenating over me, and through me. I knew I had accomplished my conquest when I entered the realm of his divine love where my heart speaks to his heart. I said, *"Lord, if you could just take me to a place in you that I could understand the why's of this life, a place in you where confusion can't find me. Lord, if you could just pick me up, and level my eyes with your eyes. Lord, if I could just get a glimpse of myself within them I know I will be alright. Lord, if you would just take me and put me on your shoulders I know I can overcome this battle that is oppressing me on every side."* As delicate tears flowed down both sides of my face I heard his gentle words, *"Amanda, if only you could see what is being birthed through these afflictions you wouldn't be afraid nor would you doubt, you would rejoice. Amanda, trust in me for I know the thoughts that I think towards you."* Sometimes it is hard to see the victory through the clouds of doubt and confusion Satan puts in front of us, but then that is where faith steps in. There have been moments that I have just wanted to run away from everything and everyone, because the battle and hurt has been so intense. I just couldn't understand. I knew I was doing everything within my power to stand, but the waves of adversity had overwhelmed me, repetitiously knocking me to the ground while my will to fight was becoming debilitated.

> *"The steps of a good man are ordered by the LORD: and he delights in his way. Though he fall, he shall not be utterly cats down: for the LORD upholds him with his hand. -Ps. 37:23"*

Jeremiah comprehended the encumbrance of just wanting to escape. Jeremiah expressed this in Jeremiah 9:2, *"Oh that I had in the wilderness a lodging place of wayfaring men; that I might leave my people, and go from them!"* David said, *"Oh that I had wings like the dove! for then would I fly away, and be at rest. See, then would I wander off, and remain in the wilderness. Selah. I would hasten my escape from the windy storm and tempest.-Ps.55:6-8"* David who stood courageously confident against Goliath while others ran in fear was now confronted with a storm he didn't want to face, yet David said, *"What time I am afraid, I will trust in you. Ps. 56:3"* Ignoring situations, people, and things doesn't make them, or the situations go away, trust me. But, when we face them with confidence and courage in God we become a champion of victory in Gods army. It is than that every impediment becomes our stepping stones into complete achievement, rather than hindering us. There is no barrier we cannot overcome when viewed through the eye of faith. So instead of viewing obstacles as insurmountable barriers keeping you from your potential, view them as challenge's that are hurdling you towards VICTORY!

> *"Now faith is the substance of things hoped for, the evidence of things not seen. -Heb.11:1"*

In 2008 during a very fragile time in my life the Lord came to my dear grandmother in a dream. In this dream my grandmother saw a storm coming in the form of a tornado and people were running everywhere looking for shelter. But, she noticed that the dark black storm clouds seemed to be bearing down upon us (my family) with intensity (there was no color in this dream everything was black and white). As everyone ran for shelter in a church basement my grandmother noticed that I didn't, but rather, I turned around and I threw my hands up in the air, I faced the storm in all its fury and as I did my grandmother said my white, sleeveless dress sparkled with beautiful pink rose buds. She said I faced this storm wtih joy, confidence, and victory. My grandmother who has been suffering with blindness for years was completely oblivious to my natural state or my spiritual state. Yet, God opened up her spiritual eyes, and allowed her to see that what I was facing was going to take courage, confidence, strength, and faith in God. God was saying, *"Amanda, Do not run."* God didn't want me to cower under fear and doubt, but rather he wanted me to face this storm with confidence. David said, *"Thou comest to me with sword, and with spear, and with a shield: but I come to thee in the name of the Lord of host, the God of the armies of Israel, who thou hast defied. 1Sam. 17:45"* David was nothing in comparison to Goliath just as I am nothing in comparison to a storm, but through God I SHALL do valiantly for it is He that will tread down my enemies. I had a word from God, a word of restoration and victory, a word of completion and upon that I stood even amid the atmosphere of doubters, and scoffers. Was my family coward for running? No. This was just a storm I had to face alone, just me and God. I had seen the cause when they didn't understand that cause. Yet, it wasn't meant for them to either. This was my storm, and as long as I understood the cause than that was all that mattered. This was a time when God was using situations, and circumstances to blossom my potential, and my purpose. He was purging my heart, and breaking my will. He was teaching me to trust him in the midst of confusion, as I yielded myself to him.

> *"For I know the thought that I think toward you, said the LORD, thoughts of peace, and not of evil, to give you an expected end. - Jer.29:11"*

Some people it seems are born with a strong confidence to achieve. They run towards their goals with such fire, determination, and confidence. While others struggle to tackle the little things, But God made each one of us different. God doesn't want us looking at what he has placed within our hands doubting or underestimating it. He doesn't want us comparing ourselves to others either. *"For we dare not make ourselves of the number, or compare ourselves with some that commend(praise) themselves: but they measuring themselves by themselves, and comparing themselves among themselves, are not wise. 2 Cor.10:12"* God says, *"Let me be your standard of measurement, not people."* God simply wants us to trust him with our lives, recognizing that he is in control. Maybe you feel like dirt, but as a preacher once said to me," *Sissy, you are dirt. You are clay in the potters."* You might feel like a speck amongst God's beautiful earth, but you are a speck that God loves abundantly.

David had strong confidence. Peter had too much. Isaiah had enough. Gideon had very little. Thomas had none, yet all were chosen by God, because God saw the embedded potential that rested within each one of them even amid the common doubts, fears, and pride we all have encountered. *"The Lord see's not as man sees; for man looks on the outward appearance, but the LORD looks on the heart. -1Sam 16:7"* God took a shepherd and made him a king (David). God took an overzealous fishermen and made him a bold spirit filled soul winner (Peter). He took a prophet with unclean lips, and made him an oracle set apart for his own purpose (Isaiah). God recognized the 'mighty man of valor' hidden under the mask of a coward (Gideon). God saw a man of honesty amid the doubtfulness of his heart (Thomas). Thomas who has often only been recognized as "doubting Thomas" was actually "honest Thomas" "humble Thomas" rather than faking faith he humbly impressed the inner doubts, and questions we all have that pride keeps us from admitting.

> For you see your calling, brothers, how that not many wise men after the flesh, not many mighty, not many noble, are called: But God has chosen the foolish things of the world to confound the wise; and God has chosen the weak things of the world the things which are mighty; And base things of the world, and things which are despised, has God chosen, yes, and things which are not, to bring to nothing things that are: That no flesh should glory in his presence. 1Cor.1:26-29"

Dwelling deep down inside of each one of us there is a treasure, it's a treasure that cannot be seen naturally, it's a unique part of us that cannot be cloned or duplicated. People may try to duplicate God's grand design, but God knows his true genuine authentic jewels. *"Behold the eye of the Lord is upon them that fear him, upon them that hope in his mercy. —Ps.33:18"* A cubic zirconia is not a real jewel and could very easily deceive me, but when viewed by the eyes of a gemologist (God) he quickly identifies if the gem is natural (God made) or synthetic (manmade imitation). A lapidary is an expert at polishing and shaping the precious stones: just as the Holy inspired word of God will polish us and shape us until we become beautiful brilliant jewels that shine for Jesus. True jewels are found embedded in gravels of stream beds, bedrock, igneous rocks (lava, magma, and fire), and alluvial gravels. Though these jewels dwell in rough rocky environments, it is there environment that is making them strong amid the element of pressure. *"But we have the treasure in earthen vessels, that the excellency of the power may be of God, and not of us. We are troubled (afflicted, or crowded) on everyside, yet not distressed (cramped); we are perplexed (puzzled, baffled), but not in despair (hopeless). Persecuted (ill-treatment or prolonged hostility), but not forsaken (abandon); cast down (feeling depressed), but not destroyed (spoiled, ruined, severe damage or attack). 2Cor. 4:7-11"* God uses hard situation to bring forth our best, the Lord said, "Amanda, I am using these afflictions in your life as a mining pick to chip away at your heart; so that the diamond that is within you can be revealed."

Before I formed thee in the belly I knew thee; and before thou camest forth out of the womb I sanctified thee, and I ordained thee a prophet unto the nations.

Jeremiah 1: 5

The Delicate Rose

As a fragile seed resting beneath the darkened soil, Unaware of the world above,
Untouched by the elements of bitterness and hurt, growing into a delicate rose bud.
As I grew the ground discharged me, as I extended myself towards the sun.
My pedals slowly unfolded, to the beautiful work you had begun.
You eclipsed my soul with you presence, preserving my life from waste.
You rain down on me with your love, refreshing my roots with grace.
Designed by Gods own craftsmanship, a masterpiece set forth in order.
Uniquely fashioned by his radiant splendor, with form correlated like no other,
Winds of doubt came swiftly, bending me beneath the woe.
Nearly uprooting my destination, tempestuous gust tossed me to and fro.
Coldness enclosed around about me, I became captured in the deadly grasp.
As hatred tried to control me, I broke free as the chains unclasp.
Storms of confusion bore down upon me, in the darkness I waited for you.
Come rescue my substance from destruction, send forth a victorious
breakthrough.
As the sun pierced through the darkness, shining down on the place I resided.
Illuminated my beauty, growth, and stability amongst a world I couldn't
confide in.
You nurtured me and you kept me, amid the uncertainties of this life.
You hid me in your secret place, away from deaths device.
Your rainbow hovers above me, awakening a promise Satan has tried to put to sleep.
Your covenant revives my soul in drought, with rains of blessing your face I seek.

By: Amanda Hagerman

CHAPTER 13

Travailing before God

From this long valley, I am watching with a heart of expectancy for the Sun (Jesus) to come bursting through these dark clouds of confusion; with rays of hope, assurance, and peace. I long for you Jesus in my hour of fear. I long to be embraced with the gentle warmth of your presence, I long to hide within the shelter of your everlasting love knowing, that everything I am, and everything I need is within you. As my tears of pain flow softly down my cheeks I make no sound but, within I am in a whirlwind of chaos and turmoil yet my confidence is surrendered fully in you. My hope is surrendered fully in you. What time I am afraid, Lord I will put my trust in you. I lean upon no man. I hope upon no man. I leave to please no man. My pillar, my hope, my existence, my life, my love, my desires, my trust, my faith, my heart is upon you, Lord.

> *"O God, my heart is fixed; I will sing and give praise, even with my glory.-Ps.108:1"*

Our tears are a message that comes straight from the heart, a message that mankind might not always understand. Our tears aren't vocal, yet they are deep inner expressions of our heart that only God can interpret. God is always standing fully armed and ready to undergird us our pain, and anguish. We can rest assured knowing we have a high priest (God) who is touched with the very feelings of our infirmities, and he is nigh unto those with a broken heart and saves those that be of a contrite spirit. God understands every fiber of our inner most thoughts. When I am broken into what seems like a thousand tiny pieces: God knows exactly how to put me back together again. He understands the core of our every situation. He knows our thoughts and the mediation of our hearts. He is moved with great compassion towards those who have faced the raging seas of life, broken, battered, beaten with the fierceness of the waves, yet have made it through with victory. "Gods thought towards us are for good and not for evil to bring us to an expectant end." God restores peace to the restless, hope to the hopeless, strength to the weak, power to the powerless, joy to the sorrowful, life to the lifeless, light to the darkness, love to those that feel unloved, companionship to the lonely, comfort to the broken, and is a father to the fatherless. Man has failed me. Friends have failed me. Family members have failed me. People have misjudged me. People have misunderstood me but God, NEVER will. Mankind is fallible, humanity is entirely unable to fathom your inner person but God the creator knows you. He knows your down-sitting and your uprising He understands your thoughts afar off. He knows you during your hour of anguish and He understands your pain. He knows what it is like to be rejected in your purpose. He knows what it is like to be betrayed by those whom you hold in high re-guard. (God fully understands you)!

> *"O lord, thou hast searched me, and known me. Thou knowest my downsitting and mine uprising, thou understandest my thought afar off. Thou compassest my path and my lying down, and art acquainted with all my ways. For there is not a word in my tongue, but, lo, O LORD, thou knowest it altogether. –Ps.139:1-4"*

Often people misunderstand tears and the purpose for them. God said, "Godly sorrow works repentance". Tears serve a purpose and without them we become hard within our hearts. God said, *"Break up the fallow ground"*. Be broken and contrite before him. Allow the Holy Spirit that is within you to break up the fallow ground of your hearts so that His word will fall on receptive soil and produce. Remember, tears aren't a sign of weakness; tears are an expression of strength. It is in our weakness that Christ is made strong. He must increase, and we must decrease. Jesus is our strength in our tears of heartache and pain, on the mountain, in the valley, victory or defeat, plenty, or little. God is unchanging and perfect for every situation.

> *"For his anger endureth but a moment; in his favour is life: weeping may endure for a night, but joy cometh in the morning. – Ps.30:5"*

I realize God desires brokenness within our inner parts. Brokenness mingled with love that brings God's people to our knee in prayer for these nations, and their leadership, *"Lord, bring us to the table of anguish that your purpose can be born within us, Amen"* Our youth, and those around about us needs to experience God's renowned power that generates life, yet God expresses his power through conduits (willing vessels). We need to be awakened with anguish, and to the crucial moment in which we are living. We need our eyes enlightened to the suffering around us, we need our hearts to be opened with compassion, and our ears inclined to the cries of the forgotten, *"Lord, break us that we might feel again. Let our hands be your hands, and to only speak as you direct us. Lord, let our actions be actions of love, and sincerity, Amen."*

> *"If my people, which are called by my name, shall humble themselves, and pray, and seek my face, and turn from their wicked ways; then will I hear from heaven, and will forgive their sin, and will heal their land. -1 Chron.7:14"*

Something that has always bothered me greatly has been those who talk of vision, and of great revelation, yet aren't willing to suffer for the cause of bringing it to perfection (It was when Zion travailed that she brought forth). I know we can't change everything, but are we really changing all that we can? Travailing before God with prayer births things in the spirit realm and we may not visually see it now, but one day we will. All it takes is a small seemingly insignificant flame (desire) to start a burning revolution for the Lord; he just requires a willing heart.

> *"I beseech you therefore brethren by the mercies of God that ye present your bodies a living sacrifice holy acceptable unto to God which is your reasonable service. And be not conformed to this world but be ye transformed by the renewing of your mind that we may prove what is that good and acceptable and perfect will of God. –Rom. 12:1"*

Let us therefore come boldly unto the throne of grace, that we may obtain mercy, and find grace to help in time of need.

Hebrews 4:16

There's a Place

I saw myself today, standing distance amongst the crowd,
Multitudes were praising God with voices clear and loud.
As I lifted my hands towards heaven, my inner voice did wail,
"Oh Lord is there a place, a place I might dwell?"
While lifting up my voice, as tears streamed down my cheeks,
I saw your glory and your splendor, as you reach out your hand to me.
Walking swiftly through the crowd, overwhelmed by your grace,
I saw the love in your eyes; I felt the warmth of your embrace.
As I stood before your throne, your glory flowed over me,
You said, "Amanda, be strong, I have a place for thee"
You placed me in the body, in the place you felt was best,
"Now stay here my child, even amid the greatest test."
Happiness was within my heart, though my tears was all I could express,
I felt swept away by your mercy, as my heart raced within my chest.
You opened my eyes to your greatness, and the importance of your love,
You have given me the wings of the eagles, with those wings I rise above.
All the chaos and confusion, all the hurt and all the pain,
All the trials and all the struggles, as I call upon your holy name.

CHAPTER 14

Reclamation of a Promise

In 2011 after Jason and I had separated; after his long hard fourteen years of battle with drugs, and alcohol; Jason finally found himself in a place that only God could get him out of. Jason had plummeted into the dark abyss of despair, and his only way out was up. David said," *I waited patiently for the LORD; and he inclined unto me, and heard my cry. He brought me up also out of the horrible pit, out of the miry clay, and set my feet upon a rock, and established my goings. –Ps. 40:1-2"* In May of 2011 Jason surrendered the battle into the hands of the Lord as he came forth weary, and wounded crawling through the doorway of mercy. The Lord took hold of his weary soul, and pulled Jason up out of the clutches of destruction. Heaven rejoiced that day with a multitude of heavenly host, but the regions of hell erupted as an angry volcano roaring out of control. Yet, I stood upon the unfailing foundation of God's written word, *"When the enemy shall come in like a flood, the Spirit of the LORD shall lift up a standard against him. –Is.59:19"* *"No weapon that is formed against you shall prosper; and every tongue that shall rise against you in judgment you shall condemn. This is the heritage of the servants of the LORD, and their righteousness is of me, said the LORD. Is.54:17"*

Even though the storm winds were sometimes great within my ears faintly I could still manage to hear, *"Amanda, I am sending restoration."* Naturally restoration seemed impossible, yet I trusted the Lord. I knew that trusting what I was feeling inside, what I was hearing around me, and what I was seeing before me, was stumbling blocks established by the enemy. There were moments that I felt somewhat like Job who said, *"For the thing which I greatly feared is come upon me, and that which I was afraid of is come unto me. I was not in safety, neither had I rest, neither was I quiet; yet trouble came. –Job 3:25-26"* All my life I carried a deep inner burden that brought me to tears before the alter of God; never knowing that one day I would embrace that very pain within my own walls. You think this is things that only happen to other people, but like my Pastor Charlie has always said, "To everybody else we are the other people." My family and I were standing amongst the ashes of what remained. So much had been stolen through the years that only a heart of faith could recover; we were in dire need of a miracle healing. It was a time of darkness; when tears became the only release I could find to channel the hurt that was flooding my soul. *"Amanda"* the Lord said, *"In the darkest moments of your life when you felt I had forsaken you, was when I was overshadowing you in my love."*

> *"He that dwelleth in the secret place of the most High shall abide under the shadow of the Almighty. I will say of the Lord, He is my refuge and my fortress: my God: in him will I trust.-Ps.91:1-2"*

People blatantly disregarded God's promise to me in disbelief just as Sarah laughed in disbelief at God's promise to Abraham. It was a tug of war within my spirit, but somehow faith always perseveres, it was like God was saying, *"Amanda, as long as you believe."* Abraham didn't stagger at the promise of God through disbelief, but was strong in faith waiting for the glory of God to manifest in his life. Jesus didn't let people's lack of confidence in him turn him away from pursuing his divine purpose, and neither should we. Jesus wasn't favored amongst the crowd. Calvary's mountain seemed to be Jesus' destination of defeat as the crowds mocked him; but it was through the pain, hurt, afflictions, weariness, tears, heartache, rejection, betrayal, and mockery that victory was conceived for all of those who believed, and would believe.

> *"He will swallow up death in victory; and the Lord GOD will wipe away tears from off all faces; and the rebuke of his people shall he take away from off all the earth: for the LORD hath spoken it. —Isaiah 25:8"*

People complicate things, because we have forgotten that Jesus turned water into wine, multiplied five loaves and two fish to feed the multitudes and parted the Red Sea for his children. People questioned Jason's salvation saying, *"The little boy cried wolf, and cried wolf until no one believed him"* and that is very true! But, one day as I was driving down the road juggling those words around in my mind. God said, *"Amanda, the little boy might have cried wolf repetitiously until no one believed him, but there came a day when he was serious!"* God said, *"Amanda, as long as Jason and I know the truth that is all that matters!"*

One night during a prayer service God showed our Pastor Charlie McGlothlin three doors. Charlie said these doors were God's blessings, and that in order for these doors to open we had to enter into them in total unity. In August of 2011 my family and I reunited after a long separation; and it seemed that I was the one having the most difficulty walking through door number one. Through the last twelve years so much trust had been replaced with dis-trust that I felt it had crippled me. It was like I was having to learn to walk again; one baby step at a time; one day at a time. Our life had been shattered by the hand of devastation, yet Jesus was picking up the shattered pieces of our lives, and creating a picture of perfection greater than that of before. He said, *"Amanda, all things are possible to them that believe."* It takes time to build something, and very little to tear it down so I acknowledged this as a work of patience within our family to bring his promise to perfection within our lives.

> *"My brethren, count it all joy when ye fall into divers temptations; Knowing this, that the trying of your faith worketh patience. But let patience have her perfect work, that ye may be perfect and entire, wanting nothing. —James 4:2-3"*

In June of 2009 Jason came home with news that he had been fired, and in November of 2011 Jason was offered his job back. In July of 1999 Jason lost his driving privileges, and now after thirteen years he is driving again. In June of 2001 we moved away from the land purchased for us, and in August of 2011 it was restored back to us. In October of 2008 division ripped through my family like a hurricane, today my family has returned to the place of love, and fellowship with one another; as the breech is slowly being repaired. We are finally starting to see the rainbow rather than the shadows of sorrow that has surrounded our domain, and all it took was stepping through the doorway of faith with courage; trusting that God knew what he was doing even when fear and confusion was present. And this is only the beginning!.

"O LORD, thou hast searched me, and known me. Thou knowest my downsitting and mine uprising, thou understandest my thought afar off. Thou compassest my path and my lying down, and art acquainted with all my ways.-Ps. 139:1-3"

For
I will
restore health
unto thee, and
I will heal thee
of thy wounds, saith
the LORD; because they called thee an
Outcast, saying, This is Zion, whom
no man seeketh after.
Jeremiah 30:17